This Rocks!

by Janette Schuster

Orlando Austin New York San Diego Toronto London

Visit *The Learning Site!*
www.harcourtschool.com

Introduction

Do you like to collect things? Beth and Kevin do. Their Aunt Justine takes them rock collecting. Aunt Justine is a geologist. A geologist is a scientist who studies Earth and its rocks.

Aunt Justine brings a small hammer. The hammer helps break big rocks into small rocks. Beth brings a hand lens. It helps her see the tiny bits that make up rocks. Aunt Justine has a pack for carrying the rocks they find.

looking for rocks

Cool Hot Rocks

Right away, Kevin sees a rock that he likes. He shows it to his aunt. "What kind of rock is this?" Kevin asks.

"That's granite," replies Aunt Justine.

"How can you tell?" Kevin asks.

Aunt Justine says that one way to tell kinds of rocks apart is by their minerals.

"All rocks are made of minerals," she explains. "Different minerals make up different rocks. Granite is made of light minerals, such as quartz. It also has dark minerals, such as mica."

melted rock

Aunt Justine explains that granite is an igneous rock. "Igneous rocks start out as hot, melted rock. You might see this melted rock flow from a volcano. In time, melted rock cools down. Then it forms solid minerals." She points to the quartz in the granite.

"I think it's pretty cool that this granite was once hot rock," says Kevin.

Bits of Rocks and Shells

Aunt Justine picks up a rock. "What do you think of this rock?" she asks Beth.

Beth says, "It doesn't look very pretty." Then Beth uses her hand lens to look closely. "Wait! I see tiny shells in this rock!"

"Those are fossils," says Aunt Justine. "Fossils are the remains of things that lived long ago. Limestone often has fossils in it. The fossils cemented together. Limestone is a kind of sedimentary rock."

limestone

"The next time I find a rock with fossils," says Beth, "I'll know that it's a sedimentary rock."

"Yes," said Aunt Justine. "Some sedimentary rocks are made of the remains of living things, like this limestone. Some sedimentary rocks are made of bits of other rocks."

Changed By Pressure

Beth points to a nearby cliff. "Wow! That rock sparkles!"

"Let's take a look," says Aunt Justine. She breaks off a piece of the rock with her hammer.

Kevin looks at the rock. "I can see light and dark minerals, like the minerals in the granite," he says.

"That's right," says Aunt Justine. "This rock has mica and quartz in it, too. But here the minerals line up in bands. This rock isn't granite. It's gneiss."

"It's 'nice'?" says Kevin.

Aunt Justine smiles and explains that gneiss is a metamorphic rock. "Metamorphic rocks form from other rocks that get buried," she says. "Heat and pressure inside Earth change the rocks to form metamorphic rocks. Often the minerals form light and dark bands, like those in your gneiss."

gneiss

Aunt Justine smiles at Beth and Kevin.

"You can learn a lot by rock collecting," she tells them. "We found three kinds of rocks today. I'll bet you can find some really interesting rocks in your back yard, too!"

As they go home, Beth says, "Thanks, Aunt Justine. I think I'll become a geologist someday, too!"